The Solitary Way

The Solitary Way

Michael Thomas

Shoestring Book Publishing, Maine, USA

The Solitary Way
Paperback

ISBN: 978-1-943974-64-1

Published by;
Shoestring Book Publishing.
Maine, USA

Copyright © 2022 By, Michael Thomas
All rights reserved.
Printed in the United States of America.

No part of this book may be reproduced, stored in a retrieval system, or transmitted in any form, electronic, mechanical; or by other means whatsoever, without written permission from the author. Except for the case of brief quotations within reviews and critical articles.

Layout and design by Shoestring Book Publishing

For information address;
shoestringpublishing4u@gmail.com
www.shoestringbookpublishing.com

Dedication

Allan and Alison have published all 24 of my books over the years. I could not have done this writing without their great help. They are responsive, suggestive and give me single attention. They are two of the best publishers I could have ever found. A writer cannot give the world his work without publishers. Thank you so much Allan and Alison. I bow deeply in gratitude.

Table of Contents

Dedication v
The Last Thing 1
time expanse 3
Recall 4
Away From Me 6
As I Age 7
an evening prayer 8
love 9
in its hands 12
Let go blindness 14
a peace in my heart 15
my charity 16
proof in the pudding 17
gone dry of happiness 18
Speaking to Jesus 19
rhyme 20
The flowers and her 24
My son 25
Please pray for me 28
life after death 29
Billy Weeks 30
no response 31
youth 32
Bobby Max 34
tears near and far 35

lots of room	36
being faulted humans	37
important thinking	38
thinking this thing through	39
I am not wise or famous	41
Ronald	42
the shoe to fall	43
complexities	44
enemies	45
whew	46
the sea	47
Thank you for reading	48
go to the dogs	49
morning	50
Norm and Gerta	51
renew me	52
A new birth	53
life goes on	54
each encounter	55
air we breathe	56
letters	57
eroticism	59
It's all about	60
eternals	62
where it happened	63
kindness	64
life	65
say that I was courteous	67

I will pray for you	68
eternal	69
Jody's got your girl and gone	71
leave it at that	73
forever	74
waiting	75
words	76
thank you	77
sacred song	78
understatement	79
regret	80
Fix yourself	81
Fuck you, to contemptible assholes	83
Questions I would ask Valsta	84
if I took her for coffee or a meal	84
Plea Psalm	87
before and after death	88
mixed up sods	89
incomplete	90
camaraderie	91
If he comes back, we will kill him again	92
a revaluation per se	95
be nice to me	97
television advertising slogans	99
We can only be human	101
she's all I adore	103
with as little pain as possible	104
repondez s'il vous plait	106

our worth and growth	107
earth plates	109
graceful forgiveness's	110
cry out of sorrow	112
no one is perfect	113
Spring comes from snow	115
We come from dust and return to it	116
prayer of patience	118
papa and the moon	119
Nocturne to love	120
Barbara Graham	121
What am I to love	122
For the thin line of fame dissolving	123
My daughter	124
Resolution of poetry	125
smooth edge of a saw	126
Gill Blaze	127
Little Winters	128
quiet self assurance	129
days of light	130
My book twenty five	131
Biography	132
Also by Michael Thomas	133

The Last Thing

I have ended my twenty fourth book
This is the first poem starting my twenty fifth book
I have not given it a name or picked the cover photo I want

I got an email from Teresa
She apologizes for not coming over
I thank her secretly for not coming over

Last time I saw her, I was amazed how old she has gotten so fast
She walks bent over and uses one of those short canes with four prong to keep steady

She has flat feet
Her hair has turned to winter snow
Her breasts are like empty bags dried out - balloons out of air

I see myself in her
I am older than her by fifteen years
Not much else to say about her
She complains that her vagina is not working properly
Her clitoris is normal and she just has never had a good hand job
Her husband is sexuality dysfunctional
It has been years since he even has touched her
He gambles all their money

The time I love Teresa the most is when we are laying naked, snuggled, and half falling asleep. That feeling is better than all the sex in the world, again and again.

I see her and her husband in church on Sunday. They sit next to each other as if they are normal and have no problems. It is a strange relationship I can't figure it out.

That is what life is: Things we cannot figure out

Someday I will run out of gas
In the future my car battery will need recharging

That is our mind: Recharging itself

This is a hell of a start for a new book
In some of my prior books I identify myself as Rabbi Schlotz
The Rabbi gets away with a lot of lies
He koshers rosaries and crucifixion's
He koshers pork
He is married to a Christian woman and sings songs to Jesus
He is irreverent and sarcastic
He is blind in one eye and deaf in the other

This is what I look like:

Just close your eyes and pray for me
It is the last thing I will remember as I die

time expanse

Forlorn
World vanished
Pathos
Past
Wood fires
Worsted wool blankets
Window curtain blowing
Insects smarter than screens
Chimneys updraft
Damper chutes partially closed
Keep heat from escaping
Iron pot taking heat to keep water ready for tea
Salt cellars
Pork keeping for holiday and holy days
Remember to give priest cookies
A thatch roof needing more twigs and leaves
Spring coming low over cottages
Church bell smelted with cast iron scraps
Ringing across dewy fields where mice perk their ears
A village enclosure so distant from skyscrapers and ages between time
horse and buggy cannot envision smoke fuming cars clanking down dirt
roads in a clamor

We wake to clean air
We wake to a rooster
We wake to fresh milk and eggs
Home baked bread scenting the air from warm oven
We wake to a mother shaking the blankets free from dust

We smile with a sun stretched as far as light can slide over silence

Recall

I am a stud
Senile
Sterile
Slouched
Like wrinkled crepe paper
Museum display bleached skeleton
Medicare specimen

Give me time
Refresh myself
In fountain of ancestors

Soldiers pass me over
Cannot reenlist
Dregs of humanity

When they call the roll
I will roll over

I once had hair
Black like ice
It has turned white
Bleached

They say age is mellow
Skin saggy sallow

I have graduated
Looks outdated
Not replicated

Out of gas
I pass

Loose change

Angels said
It's a pity
Once spiffy
Now dizzy

First born
Scorned

Away From Me

I am removing you from my address book
I will no longer respond to your emails
It is not that I hate your or are angry
I just do not need to associate with you
You are a person who takes and does not give
A person who does not know how to thank

I have ran across others like you
Others who never last long as a friend

I will tell you something you may have heard but never followed:
Treat others as you want to be treated

Jesus said on the cross:
Father forgive them for they know not what they do

Socrates drank the hemlock knowing he was faultless

You do not know who you are
Never once have you asked me if I need anything

Your asking me for money is an addiction you have
Your life is not centered and you turn
to an easy way to solve your problems

I feel no sorrow for you, since your life is not mine
I wish you well, but I wish you no harm, just away from me

As I Age

Further from mind is closer to heart
Heart is best friend when in need
Bach reaches into our soul
Beethoven takes us on a merry go round
Shostakovich composes against restraints
Tchaikovsky makes us understand lesbianism
Picasso twists us into a pretzel of images

When we reflect it is with sweet savor of pathos
It is a fool who thinks themselves wise
Wisdom is subtle, it lies below all our realities

Aftermath of emotion is silence
Silence is the space between words
Mozart said that the space between notes
 was more important than the notes

If I offer you my grace, you can feel my charity
Let all those who have known me speak in my favor
I have a hole where understanding awoke me to my faults
Words are useless to a true poet

I am in favor of nothing
and promises of a future fade as I age

an evening prayer

I pray for my mother and father
Whose sacrifice help me farther

My brother and two sisters
For him love, them assisters

Ex-wife mother of my children
Estranged but heart not hidden

My lovely daughter jewel forever
First born, fed, rocked to deliver

My son I assist with all I can do
His gifts and faults, he is me too

A partner who makes me wealth
I wish her and family good health

Neighbors known or site unseen
Wish them all the best of dreams

You readers who comment, read
I am grateful for good will I need

A god I sense but never conceal
Belief in full faith that I can feel

Please take this prayer in trust
I do my best as always I must

love

Shakespeare Sonnet 116
Let me not to the marriage of true minds
Admit impediments. Love is not love
Which alters when it alteration finds,
Or bends with the remover to remove:
O, no! it is an ever-fixed mark,
That looks on tempests and is never shaken;
It is the star to every wandering bark,
Whose worth's unknown, although his height be taken.
Love's not Time's fool, though rosy lips and cheeks
Within his bending sickle's compass come;
Love alters not with his brief hours and weeks,
But bears it out even to the edge of doom.
    If this be error and upon me proved,
    I never writ, nor no man ever loved.

Think that love is a marriage? With impediments?
Love changes everything especially when it ends.
Confusion ensues for years even forever in doubt.
People who join together have diametric opposition.
One is weak and one strong. Upon finality the weak
person sinks into depression and the strong one stays superior.

The whole idea of love is to combine a needy person with a fulfilled
person. The strong person uses the weak person for confidence.
Usually the lessor person is mocked or made fun of.

Love is a term denoting temporary union. Love never ever lasts. All of
life is an endeavor to combine elements in an attempt to raise a lower
and maintain or raise up an upper force.

Love is a teeter totter and only one wins by weight
to keep the other in the air and helpless.

An insignificant person will keep their fault forever.
A person of significance will increase their advantage as time ensues.

It is a romantic fallacy that love is forever.
Truth is that time will have out and both contestants
will decrease or increase based upon their original positions.

Love's corollary is hate.

In between is a mass of contradictions
that gives one favor and the other a prisoner to their natures.

I have never had a situation where I came out ahead
from caring for another person.

When I care too much the other person takes advantage of me.

Love is a situation of war and one side
will always come out the winner,
with the other side the loser.

Besides the definition of love is multifaceted.
There is physical love, emotional love, essential love, false love,
advantageous love, and so many other types: on-and-on.

Even if a union is arranged by others - such as marriage for advantage
politically (per se): One side may grow to like or dislike the other, but
that is irrelevant since dispositions weigh-in of very lessor meaning.
 It is the balance between two people that matters most.

My grandmother had an arranged marriage to join two vineyards
together. Her husband never lived with his young bride but gave her ten
children without paying for anything. He would show up at night,
impregnate her, and leave before the morning came.

She was too weak to deny him.

She worked all her life as a char laborer
and paid for the children on her own.

The love between them was obviously
 one of a weak person under the thumb of a strong person.

My grandfather was very rich and my grandmother poor.

I will tell you what I think of love: It is a contradiction in terms of definitions. Even god loved Satan, but to his dismay, his love for the fallen angel was a disappointment and as Michael, the archangel, drove Satan out of heaven: God shed a tear and waved goodbye to the devil.

in its hands

And time keeps itself inside a vacuum of secret chambers
Like a pyramid with crevices containing a maze of thoughts

Where grave robbers go away without finding what they seek
Time seals itself into memories of love that please the mind

And love is a word we use for lack of a better god or angels
Love that defines itself with forgiveness

Failure of not loving has its own penalty
I cannot love you because I am imperfect

Trust me, I am loving you as best I can
I crawl into bed and warm myself as seasons pass

I dangle my arms and shift my weight to get comfortable
I try hard to empty my mind and let sleep take itself seriously

We wish for sleep to not end
We want to wake so refreshed that we are born again

I cannot change the past but I can change the future

Time

Time is an elusive conundrum
Time is love
Love is time

Time and time again I go over my life
and find mysteries that I can never solve

Like a bird who is not aware of time,
I sing and try to find a match for my loneliness

I live in a time of sorrow
I live in pathos
I am half-finished and will die that way
I will enter Valhalla a pilgrim of innocence

I will leave heaven and start a new time to love
I will part with angels who protect me
and only hope they will keep watch over me

Yesterday I loved you and tomorrow I will try again
I wash my hands and scrub my face of visions

Like a slave to fate, I turn on a wheel of reminiscences
Let me be who I am, please god

You are not any more perfect than me
You could not even create perfect angels

Satan is your opposite
Like King Arthur, your son will live to kill you

Mordred is your Oedipus who will slay you
and sleep with his mother
I cannot be my father but I can pray for him
I cannot be my mother but I can learn from her:

Patience
Love is waiting
Like Godot love never comes
Simple truth is love

        Love is truth
        Truth is love
        We can only let the mystery follow its path
        and we are in its hands

Let go blindness

Sun not alabaster
Nor earth ochre
Drenched rainbows
Oil slicks
Mirror melodies
Avalanche of:
Rock slide rubies
God's shone pebbles

Eyeful diadem
Flickering beneath a sudden stream
Rivulets of choral trickles

A star brilliance
Caught in a hurricane of colors

Waking to a deceitful cadence
Chrome stretched calliope

Magical malevolence
A jeweled experience
Doppler ribbon waves

We are mesmerized
Tolerant toward light
Burnt blasphemy
Labeled innocence
Let go blindness

a peace in my heart

When John Field nocturnes sound right
All things in place with bills paid
Enough money to relax

So many books written and published
Relationships with family and friends are okay

I remember being told that maybe I was waiting for a shoe to fall

I will shut my eyes and let sleep work its magic
I will wake and follow my plans for the ensuing day

If disaster is to come, I am unaware of it
I thank the spirits that watch over me
I am eighty one years old and have outlived all my enemies

My remembrance will be that I tried to be as kind as possible
And, I wish readers and those that will never read this:
A peace in your heart like mine

my charity

Reality

What we perceive

How we act based upon our belief systems

There seems to be various layers of what is truth
Accepted conducts change depending on situations

If you are Henry eight you can kill people
and create your own church to get what you want

If you are Alexander the great you burn villages and conquer
If you are Socrates you drink hemlock

I have a church lady who sits with her husband and pretends

She has no compunction to have an extramarital affair
to relieve the tedium of her marriage

I have refrained from physical intimacies
for over forty years and I have no regrets

My life is complete and I am secure with what I accept

Yet the world changes with climates, governments, wars and possible meteors striking earth

I will tell you what is correct: Let things happen and protect yourself by doing as much good as possible every day

In the end my charity will comfort me as I live and die

proof in the pudding

Do you think your smarter than men?
Fool them into thinking they are superior?

Pretend that your libido has been satisfied?
Let them think they are better workers than you?

They work, eat, sleep.
They do not keep the cupboard organized.

They do not do the laundry.
Vacuum, clean toilets and sinks.
Earn more than you.
Have no idea how to keep a budget or handle the money.

My mother controlled the world around my father.
She made the deals and moved to three houses without his help.

When it came time to retire she said to him: If you think your going to sleep with me all day long, you are wrong.. Go out and get a part time job and leave me alone.

When he died, she was amazed that he had passed on her getting his retirement benefits.

Women sew, darn, keep things moving smoothly.
Men lay exhausted atop their wives after sex and she waits to roll him off before he sleeps.

Do you think you are the superior race?
Well the proof is in the pudding.

gone dry of happiness

Oh! I have loved
Soft nipple breast fleshy
Squeezed between fingers
Tightening
Rigidity of skin
Eyes closing

Expectation increasing
For fingers inside her chamber of peach sliced
for birthing screams

We have been tied together
Her Eve apprehension beneath my boulder heavy corpse
Our blending like butter melting between our hearts

I have loved in series of situations
Each woman with same face

I have dreamed drowsy
Her hopes she succeeded
"Was it good for you?"
Approval of her fingers relaxed

We all have loved as a testament to our children
Who replace us on an earth gone dry of happiness

Speaking to Jesus

Speaking to Jesus

I tell him of tomato soup in cans

Buddha interrupts by burping
Jesus says: God bless you
Buddha repeats his burps and says: Thank you.

I tell Confucius that I have a hard time loving my neighbor
and my country
He says: I had the same problem and so I moved to Australia

Achilles says that rumors of Odysseus reaching home, might be true
Penelope was interviewed by BBC
and she showed her burial shawl she kept weaving
and unweaving to avoid suitors

Circe sent an email to "whom it may concern":
Please write, you know who I am and I miss you

Word got out that Dido committed suicide as Aeneas sailed away to Italy. All the wedding invitations were tossed in the trash. She requested that Aeneas's sword be given back to him if he ever comes back to Carthage. She told her servants to wipe the blood clean. Virgil was typing furiously to get his book to the publishers.

While all this was going on, Helen (of Troy) was smiling as Menelaus hefted her over his shoulder and took her to his ship where she complained that she wanted clean sheets and coffee in the morning.

Lastly, Alexander the great, just as he died, reminded his men to make the mortgage payment on his mother's house and continue her pension. All the lands he conquered went up for sale including buildings, mines and drilling rights. Stock trading took an upswing as soldiers moved to take advantage of land deeds.

rhyme

She walks with me in majesty
Her radiance is bright to see
Like we two have linked destiny
Bound entwined root to tree

Both of us have passed through
Where living legends who knew
Differences to stop or take que
Where shadows of eagles flew

I am her counterpart and link
Sacred wine only priests drink
Thoughts wise people think
Who disappear in one blink

This life is short at both ends
To regret or to make amends
Reasoning or just pretends
No direction as the road bends

I have memories will not die
Lasting tears I always cry
Burning desire to reach high
A pyramid pointed to the sky

No letter poem or song sung
No ladder climbing last rung
No valley chapel bell rung
Yet maypole banners slung

I reach end of words rhyme
Limits to sun-stretched time
Parading in a mirror mime
Exchanging dollar for a dime

I am not a criminal or a saint
A wise person is what I ain't
Shadow with a powder taint
Vanishing point artists paint

So wish me well go your way
Know yourself how to pray
Yesterdays become today
A corpse exhumed on a tray

Cowboy buried with his boot
Robber dying with no loot
A horn that will not toot
Invisible silent voice mute

Last but not least
Late to the feast
Rabbit not beast
Compass's east

Sun comes up, sun goes down
Circus show without gay clown
Earth sea blocks out the brown
Country bumpkin leaving town

We all have missions to attain
In days bright or days of rain
Health or sickness such pain
We fall short counting all gain

Little does the prophet know
Seeing events come and go
Drawn out as angels in snow
Hurling kites with tail in tow

A bird in the bush, one in hand
As lemonade tastes so bland
Meaningless as wedding band
Soldier denounced for a stand

A little less a little more
Where waves find shore
Heaven opens up a door
Devil knocks us to floor

Angels rescue wayward souls
As only sinner prays or knows
Ahab waving as whale blows
A farmer plants his life in rows

A city takes all land and water
Till life is unsustainable-harder
In the end no goods can barter
Mom, Dad, Son and daughter

If you wait for something to end
Keep eye on how things blend
A shepherd has sheep to tend
A tailor, sock holes to mend

A builder uses his plumb
Teachers take one dumb
Hopes knowledge succumb
To soften hearts once numb

Little can we count or trust
When a river dam will bust
Or true love becomes lust
Wood ages, metal does rust

Time will pass as we sleep
Oceans keep secrets deep
A widow needs to weep
Misers love all they keep

A buccaneer will walk the plank
The foil Hotspur plays his prank
Pilgrims have their god to thank
Military give themselves rank

Storms sink ships at sea
Prison inmate makes a plea
English gentry sip their tea
Lowing herds wind over lea

Before we end, think it thru
Being Christian or Jew
Pagan or killer who slew
The enemy who flew

A story has character and plot A
stormy sea or Gordian knot A
garment with a bloodstain spot A
victim dead from a gunshot

Breakfast and orange juice
Before your hung with noose
Rope is tight never loose
You are a real dead goose

At the end of every story
Is a finale so very gory
That no fame or no glory
Could fill up its vast quarry

The flowers and her

July day lilies fade

Invasive wild butterscotch lilies I root up and discard
It is the designer lilies I like the best

They bloom for one day and you must snip them after they bloom
in order to give the plant energy to produce more

They spread as long as you keep the wild ones from taking over
In July they bloom the best

I would follow her with a receptacle to trash or recycle the dead ones
She allowed me to build and weed all her gardens
I would watch her hands as she used her fingernails
to cut off the finished buds

I loved her hands as much as I loved the flowers
Her hands were a combination of wild and designer fingers.
They were long like her feet

I loved her feet and took every opportunity to massage them with her
socks off

She is dead like the daylilies and I only have her memory to sooth me
She died of so many things: Her shaking, her diabetes, her veins clogged

The last I saw her she was in a coma in a hospital bed
and non-responsive

I wiped her forehead and sad a prayer over her
The nurses asked if I needed anything. I thought to ask if they could
bring her back to life for maybe a few hours and I could say all the things
that I never said to her or the daylilies before time closed their lives out:

The flowers and her.

My son

Of course I love my son
My daughter ignores me

Differences between my son and myself,
against the world, are pronounced

Differences between my son and myself are extremely varied
Main difference is he is a constrictive person
and I am a very expansive person

His realities are limited, mine are unlimited
My son has Aspers Syndrome and does not know it

His condition is something
never been discussed by his mother and myself

I discovered it years ago from a lady
who observed him and revealed it to me

I was dumfounded that I never saw it on my own
But, since I now know it,
I keep getting indications of how true it is

Mostly, I have come to love him stronger
since all the behavior he exhibits,
I have come to understand.

He repeats himself
He never comes to a topic clearly

He was caesarian C-section born
and never had to struggle to come into the world

When he was born he physically was perfect,
unlike his sister,
who had to really struggle for over fourteen hours to be born

He is not adept as using tools whatsoever
He does not even own a screwdriver or pliers

He is not gay,
but he does not have any sexual relationships with women or men

Funniest thing he does,
is leave things scattered about a room when he enters:
Like his keys here, his hat there, his jacket somewhere else
and his backpack in another place

When he leaves he forgets something
and I have to scan the room
to remind him to take everything with him

He does not pay attention to people when they say something.
He will ask a waitress over and over the same question

He owns five junk used cars that stink from previous owners so bad that
I will never be a passenger in his cars or I will get sick from the smells

His low grade sickness is Autistic but he can function adequately
His sister is an accomplished school teacher

He has a college degree in legal assistant
and he can speak Spanish but he never uses his credentials

He has worked all his life as a door guard
for St John's hospital in Ypsilanti
He has never missed a day of work
and seems to please his bosses

He is an extreme recycler and his car has boxes and boxes of cans
and bottles that he hoards and never seems to get rid of

He will stop and pick up old mattress springs
and discarded trash from everywhere

I never ask him to take my small bags of trash to the dumpsters,
since he will go through each of my bags with a fine tooth comb
to recycle everything I throw away

This is my son who never reads books or considers psychological issues
I cannot even carry on a discussion with him

Lastly, he is a kind and generous person whom I have come to love
greatly, despite all the impairments to his character

Please pray for me

I get so tired of Patricia
My dog nose sniffing up her ass

My stupid following her from one life to another
She is always married to someone else when I find her

I cannot seem to get over my blind innocence, since she is always in it for money and she loves to play me along without ever really loving me

She loves to make fun of me: Ridicule me: Laugh at my miscues;
 Use me as a butt of her jokes.

I am a pig headed fool
There is an insecurity within me that guides me improperly

She is Slavic
She always has big breasts that she lets me touch

If we get naked she wants me to rush and ejaculate fast to get it over with

All I want to do is cuddle with her
and she is impatient to get back with her husbands

When I am alone and reflecting upon the situation,
 I feel so foolish

She disturbs my dreams and waking hours
No other women can compete with my attraction I feel toward her

There is no doubt that I am a dolt and a donkey mentality
This is my life, always giving her all my money and fixing things for her
I feel caught within a circle of behavior that I can never change

Please pray for me

life after death

Things I will never forget
Day I realized god at age six
Day President Kennedy was shot

Day of 1964 9.2 magnitude earthquake in Alaska on March 28
when ground swayed and I got queasy and dizzy

Day of mortar attack when Murphy got killed / Hearing grown men
calling for their mother as they died

Day I flew out of Vietnam and the airplane accelerated on takeoff
and went almost straight up to avoid ground fire from the Viet Cong

Day my two children were born and day I left my marriage
and those children behind - saddest day in my life facing my failure
at in institution that never fit my solo lifestyle

How I dealt with a wife who was too immature
and with whom I had no communication with
Day Carolyn left me and I tail-spin into depression for over seven years

Day I found Patricia and with her help climbed out of the black hole
passing the CPA exam, starting my business and fluctuating between
wealth and poverty, ultimately being given money to be comfortable

I will never forget all the twenty five books I had published.
Grand fame eluded me, but it did not matter
because creating so many books was edifying and stupendous.

So many memorable occasions.
My small insignificant life with things history would scoff at.
But, here I am alive at eight two years old and managing
to outlive all my enemies who I will see again
when I pass through the veil
 and arrive at life after death

Billy Weeks

Billy Weeks
Heard begging
No such person
But, we all hear him going on and on
Billy Weeks moaning like some creature ain't never human

Some said he rode too fast and spun out
Lost control at night on a curve
Never walked again. Wheel chair bound

Katy left him
He moved back into his ma and pa home
Cried every night
Could not be consoled

We all listen
But we give pause to ghosts or a devil needing rescue

Billy Weeks janitor who left to buy bread and never came back
Never married / Never divorced
King of a boxer
Street fighter

If we find him, he is got a drinking habit
Where is he? We find his bed empty
There is no chair or place for him on holidays
or fall during the seasons change

Billy Weeks announced as the loser
Due to circumstances we had no part in
Billy the town crier
Seen him lately?

We ordinarily would not bother you,
but he left hoping someone put him out of his misery

Michael Thomas

no response

Not sure if there will be much more than this
I feel shame writing about something involving her

At first I lay with her and little-by-little
her clothes came all off under a blanket

She always lays face down
Rarely did I see her face
She made no noises or exaggerated breathing
She made no indication or response as I touched her

I am not sure how a neighbor suspected something
and began a private inquiry
He was like a priest in demeanor
Somehow he began a series of incidents with the girl

He started reading poems to her
She never spoke to him

There was one poem that aroused her
A poem about a woman holding orgasms in her heart

I forgot to tell you that I spent much time
fingering her vagina as she lay still
I am not sur how this story will end
I am sure there is more to tell

This is not a confession

This is more like we looked into a window
but had no control over what we saw

The only control was the ongoing intimacy that we had as she lay immobile and acquainted to my fingering her with her not acting or responding

youth

His son never left home at age fourteen

He never set pins at Parkside bowling alley

Nor ever unloaded semi-trucks at Big Bear supermarket (now defunct)

Returned empty carts to Wrigley supermarket (renamed)

Or taped huge sale notices to the window as he flirted with Frances Marie Louise De Ponio who giggled in her white Avery Baking Company uniform so tight that her tits bulged out demonstratively

Frances Mari Louise would coy bashfully as he played with her breasts in the front seat of the 1950 Dodge fluid drive with the grey velour smooth seats

At this tender age,
life was full of wonder and experiences waiting to unfold

How can Rabbi Schlotz explain to the world how he saw unlimited visions waiting to happen

He spend hours in quiet libraries like Mark Twain branch on Gratiot Avenue inside the oak smell paneling walls of silence as he read book after book

Or the hallowed halls of the Detroit Public Library main branch with the ornate colonnade Greek arched entrance

It was as if Rabbi was an emperor of his own kingdom

Neither his son or daughter could imagine the depth of their father who singlehandedly slew dragons or rode with King Arthur through Avalon to the edge of a sea stretched into infinity

The ignorance of innocence portending events is this child of history who slept with dreams untold

My son whose story could be written on a matchbook cover would never have a life needing volumes of words to describe it

Along Mack Avenue Rabbi would walk with Michael Patrick Dennis Haag and the two of them stopping at the Bakery where Michael's aunt would give them free donuts

As simple as life was being an altar boy serving mass with father Vismara

Receiving holy communion as if it really was the body and blood of Jesus

Going to De-Bucks corner grocery store and sitting on the steps eating Hostess chocolate donuts and drinking milk out of plastic containers as a reward for getting up so early to assist the priest

Bobby Max

Find me a Bobby Max who does rap
His hair turning grey under a knit cap

A black dude with a greasy dirt face
Lives in a motel has no regular place

Momma says she ain't see him at all
If you come across him tell him call

Angie: His last known divorced wife
Shows how he cut her with his knife

Has a deep scar under his left eye
Hangs at Effie's Grill loves peach pie

Owes Louie the Deuce much dough
For coke and taking too much blow

Not much else to tell you: No reward
Lots of us want him dead on a board

tears near and far

Humans want tenderness
Want their insides to vibrate with good feelings

Crotches sensitive aroused
Sex gods way of furthering species

All creatures are mindless reproductive vehicles
Thinking is not a part of intercourse

Whales, elephants, dogs, fish become tranced during the act of survival
War is a condition of being in a comma of killing

Thoughts are clouded during the taking of life or the furtherance of life
Most cogent words are: "Father forgive them for they know not what they do"

Rene Descartes could have said:
I am a thing that thinks without thinking

"What the hell is wrong with you?
 Didn't you think of what you were doing?"

Odysseus had to be tied to his ship mast
 to not be lured by the sirens song
Circe was goddess of necromancy and illusion.
She lured Odysseus with a spell that only Hermes could break to free him

Odysseus I miss you in my boudoir
We could have raised the old bar
Take me riding in the car car
Hole in one just below par
Gone to heaven as a star
Look at where we are
Choked with catarrh
Tears near and far

lots of room

I come from a city
No straw roosters
Cement not hay
Veteran boosters

A parish priest
Rows of houses
City streets neat
Girls in blouses

Nature smells nay
No hawks circle
Squirrels at play
Fences to hurdle

Temperature hotter
Than airy valleys
Houses together
Dirty junk alleys

Cops are often
Sirens blare
Asphalt soften
In urban air

Long for forests
Where buds bloom
Birds in chorus
Lots of room

being faulted humans

I used to be there
Where?

Where I was not known
Been anonymous all my life

Better to avoid acclaim
Keeps one sane

I watch prominent people get lost in their fame
They lose touch with what is proper

They begin to believe the lies like the emperor
who thought he had clothes

Hemmingway, Achilles, Odysseus, Hitler, Stalin, William Kotzwinkle -
they and more others, all got driven off center by their confoundedness

I am here
Where wind blows / sun goes / snow cold / fall knows
Secret to balance is to wobble a lot
We never are true prism because north keeps moving its magnet

Do not kid yourself:
Believe none of what you hear and all of what you cannot see
Secrets to semblance are hidden

Best we can do is to forgive others
and ourselves for being faulted humans

important thinking

The New World Imagined

India
China
Russia
United States
Others
  Australia
  Bill Gates
  Elon Musk Tesla
  Zuckerberg
  Jeff Bezos Amazon
  Warren Buffett
  Bernard Arnault
  Universities
  Other Others

Issues
  health
  education
  environment climate
  financial
  economic
  space

thinking this thing through

People who left this for you did you a disservice

Ah.........

No Ah's about it. It was just plain mean what they did. I sensed it, when I first heard it and I knew, you, Course I didn't know whoever you was, was in for it. But here we are and now I hear tell your name is:

Bill.....

Yea, Bill, listen: I'll try to splain it to you, so just be patient since I, here, am not too good at this.

See: there was three things you had to deal with: Regular insurance, Conditional insurance and case of disaster insurance.

Yea.........

Be patient. This here conditional thing was based on how much labor you had and what kind of labor it was. See: If here was labor in danger of injury than that there insurance would be lots higher than you would think or wish for. Regular insurance is cut-n-dry. It don't change much cause its based on values of property. Like, let me give you an example:

If-n you own a building, they is a an assessment issued that is equal to other buildings near yours. You, of course, have the right to argue against what they say your assessment is.

Okay.......

Darn near simple that all things are equal and buildings are all pretty much the same.

Now here is the problem when we get to the conditional insurance: You are forced to pay a deposit that could go up or down - mostly up, in favor of the policy issuers. Before we go on, would you like a cup of coffee?   Doris, bring Bill a coffee. You like cream and sugar?

Double........

Double it is. Doris bring Bill a couple of them white sugar donuts with a napkin.

Thing I forgot to tell you is that you got to get a signed paper from the worker saying whether or not they will pay for their own insurance coverage. It gets deeper. If the worker gives you a paper stating that they are covering their own insurance, then you are taken out of the picture and you do not owe any conditional insurance. Remember, it all depends on that worker taking responsibility for their own insurance.

I told you it would be a mess thinking this thing through.

I am not wise or famous

I am not sure realty is what I see or understand
I am surrounded by divergent viewpoints
Left, right - I remain silent in a center of controversy
When we are poised between Sigmund Freud
and Carl Jung we sit contemplative
We are unable to find peace with either
The best I come away with is that Jung affirms pre-knowledge
in the soul before birth through language skills

This understanding coincides with reincarnation which refutes
established beliefs of heaven or hell
I find it difficult to believe in a permanent place of joy or punishment
Mark Twain says: Most people can't bear to sit in church for an hour on
Sunday. How are they supposed to live somewhere very similar to it for
eternity?

I find it more believable in being reborn over
and over to correct our misunderstandings
Freud says that if you are born with defects your only hope
is to rid them through therapy
Jung says you rid them through repeating lives
Jesus hints at reincarnation by saying that one needs
to be born again to enter into heaven

The Egyptian belief systems has the soul being weighed
against a feather to determine judgement
King Arthur is poised to come back to revive the land / Jesus
is poised to come back a second time
Darwin Bedford from Canada says: If Jesus returns, kill him again
I am not clever
I am not famous
Hardly anyone listens to me

But, I truly thank you for reading or considering this
inconsequential writing

Ronald

Ronald you have to leave this building
and take your step daughter with you

The two of you are the worst neighbors I have ever had

You own a gun that you showed me.
You are too emotional to have a gun.

You are a crook who stole the purchase
of your second unit from me.
You knew I had an offer pending

You and your daughter do not ever help me with groceries
for over eight years.
I am eighty one and have a hard time getting up the stairs to my unit.

You and your daughter turned me into the police
for checking the mail in my long t shirt

You speak out loud how you do not like looking at my ass, yet,
Shakespeare says: "Me thinks the man doth protest too much"
Meaning that I believe you are gay talking about my ass too much.

You and your daughter never thank me for giving things to you

I do not know that else to tell you.
Leave and go somewhere else away from me
and the good people in this building

the shoe to fall

My life is in order
I have decided to not aggravate
my next door neighbor

He is not worth the wasted energy
My bills are all paid

My relationships are balanced
My work is caught up

My health is holding
I have the best movies to watch

My computer is working as well as it can be
staying away from viruses
I am doing what someone said:
Do not wait for the shoe to fall

complexities

In came spring
With death in disguise

Out of earth
Green flower surprise

Whisper of wind
Floating butterflies

Colors that melted
Birds announce cries

Ocean shores littered
Ships tattered ties

Wishes of summer
A hot tepid prize

Fear not leaves falling
For even god dies

Change crosses forests
Autumn colors subside

We breathe through scarfs
In winter we improvise

Seasons switch venues
As we live time just flies

enemies

Key to life is to get even
People who are cruel deserve retribution
Outliving enemies is one way
Making a success out of yourself is a great equalizer
Sometimes it is the hidden aspects of life that makes one superior
My enemies do not know they are pitted against me
Know thyself and know thine enemy
Count your friends as few
Count your enemies as many
Funny when we remain anonymous to each other,
we make better enemies to each other
Forgive us our trespasses as we forgive those who trespass against us
Father forgive them for they know not what they do
On the field of battle, all is fair
My dad used to say: Be slow and walk up to your enemy.
When you get close enough, kick them right in the balls
My dad was a fighter
I always avoided fights
In my whole life, I never got in a fight on the streets
I balanced things in my mind before I enacted revenge
Love thy neighbor as thyself and love god with thy whole heart
and soul I try to let others pass me up because I know
that somewhere, down the road, I will pass them
The key to life is to consider oneself attempting to becoming enabled
The key to life is to remember that you will never become perfect
The key to life is to accept your incompleteness
Life is a process of defeating your internal enemies
Heaven is false. The future is what we strive for by doing good
and avoiding your enemies

whew

Secretly I am a Jew
Hitler left us so few

Wild winds blew
Air fresh and new

Where "oy vey" grew
Jesus Christ knew

Apostles his crew
Our religions grew

Bigotry took its cue
Horses gave us glue

Where all truth flew
Into morning dew

The devil just knew
How to bug-a-loo

Leonardo Da Vinci drew
Making Mona Lisa true

Do not start to sue
Whatever you do

Humanity's in a stew
Soon, we will die too

the sea

Buried beneath seas
Ghosts of sailors
Ships broken
Homes for innocent fish
Algae encrusted fossilized
All banners and singing on shore muted against turbulent waters
We come from the sea
We go back to the sea
There is no victory for men suffocated
Men breathing last bits of air before they expire
Sir Frances Drake weaving in and out of the Spanish Armada in victory
German submarines futile in stopping Allied ships
We wiggle ourselves through centuries to grow legs and arms from fins
The sea is a banquet of non survivors
Great whales tip ships capsized
My wife and children wait inconsolable on land for me to never return
Great icebergs laugh at our ships
Our callous heating of the atmosphere causes ice to melt
and seas to rise to drown us
The myth of a Noah flood suddenly becomes a reality
The wolf pack of history rises from depths and great choral waves welcome them back
Take no comfort in a Darwin for we will lose ourselves as centuries take away our legs and arms and cast us back into the sea to start all over again in secret caves where flagella waves us to sleep
We either freeze, are burned to death or drown, take your pick
When spaceships take us off the earth,
we will go to planets that have oceans

Thank you for reading

I leave restaurant to drive home
I had French onion soup and onion rings
My stomach is about sixty percent okay and my bad tooth is quiet
I back the car watching for traffic
The girl who passed walking has disappeared into one of the shops
I pull forward and reach the entrance to the busy main street
Entering onto the turn lane I make sure to merge and head home
Now, I am single, but I can imagine that I have a wife
waiting for me at home

She has long thin fingers, a well rounded ass and nice tits.
She is not greatly intelligent, but what can you do,
(even for a make believe consort)
I pretend that she will greet me as I enter my home
She will smile and kiss me gently
I live alone for over fifty years and I am not lonely but I imagine things
For fifty years I have had no woman come to me
So, here I am home and Teresa is still at work in the restaurant
I get comfortable and prepare a pipe to smoke
Life is funny
I will watch more of a video and then go to sleep
Thank you for even listening to this and reading

go to the dogs

A dog is a dog
Cat is a cat
All creatures, along with their neighbor plants, can feel: pain or joy
Neither of them can write an essay describing their experience
They can feel wind blow but cannot build a spaceship to determine how, what, where when or why
They cannot chose between salad dressing and mayonnaise
They are unable to put gas in their cars which they do not own anyways
You will never hear of a creature graduating from high school or joining
a military service
Even though we humans have peers
Our personalities are different
My next door neighbor is a dog

He is allowed to sign a lease: Live in his unit:
And play rock and roll music
His family never explored
The Love for Three Oranges by Sergei Prokofiev
I do not feel sorry for him, his family or the dogs
he keeps penned in a cage outside his doorway

In fact I believe they all are better off the way they are
I just encourage my daughters to not marry into their families,
despite the fact that they both listen to the same album
of Prince's music: Purple Rain
I have o guard against feeling superior
In fact I believe I am better off being the way I am
My feet still hurt, as theirs do
My eyes need to close in a dust gust of wind, as theirs do
But their heart will never be broken by hearing Tchaikovsky's Francesca da Rimini played by Leonard Bernstein and the New York Philharmonic (circa 1970)
The world around me can all go to the dogs

morning

Sky cracks open
An egg cooking
Glisten

Sun exposes
Its hiding place
Beneath a moon
of fading alabaster

Night surrenders
A prisoner in hiding
Incognito
In shame

Little do we dream
of shadows serene
Where flowers welcome
Rays of magnanimous grace

Let us wake
Stand looking out of our windows

God sees us and removes his cautions
Morning arrives on golden chariots

Norm and Gerta

It was decided to disconnect the tubes and let Norm die
His wife, Gerta, fainted when the doctors pronounced him dead
She never recovered and a double funeral was planned
Porky, the dog, sat on the porch watching the door expecting
Norm to come out soon

When they took Norm and Gerta to the burial site in the local cemetery,
they used the old Oldsmobile and left the trunk open to accommodate
the single casket hanging out
It had been decided to place both bodies into one extra large casket
to save money
The driver, Bernie, an old friend of the family.
was given the vehicle by the surviving family
Bernie thought how Norm was a miser but he never spoke it
In his mind, Berne pictured old Norm's hand awakened
and reaching for a five dollar bill
that might be waved overhead. He giggled quietly
At the memorial meal a sparse dish of chicken
and potatoes was served and attendees paid for their own drinks
Norm and Gerta were buried with one head stone. Lynn, their only
child, kept a handkerchief in her pocket as prayers were read. She
decorously threw a handful of dirt over the descent box with a clang and
a single mourner threw a flower after

There was a slight cast of rain darkening the sky
as they drove away and observers mentioned how eerie the air felt
Nobody noticed how the flowers over the grave wilted immediately
after the mourners left the grounds

renew me

I will die carrying with me
Inside my genetic soul
Characteristics of sin
Elements of sainthood

A mitigated sovereign
Of similitude
I will be carried to the gates of hell
And if I burn, then be it
I will be carried to the gates of heaven
And if I am admitted, then be it
My long for search for balance
Will leave me tottering between extremes

Give me peace
Or neurotic gods
Solace from pathos
Cut me loose from hunger, lust, avarice, sloth, pride, ego
Let me float free of pain and anger

I fear nothing but solitude
In silence I will hear truth
Oh! Gods of horrific war
Give me back my arms
Restore my eyes
Renew my hope
In love

A new birth

I am in a hurry to die
To return for another try
I will tell you the truth not lie
I am old and ready for the old by-and-by

My body has run out of gas
Racings no good I cannot last
My enemies are dead asleep in the past
There is no joy I am late even for midnight mass

Let the ax take off my head
Machine gun me I have nothing to dread
My blood is dried, it is no longer cardinal red
One casket said to the other: Is that you coffin?

The memory of all that I have done
Is forgotten and gone like the setting sun
The angels laugh and tell me to slow down, don't run
My poems are all dirges or reduced to being boring puns

So wave me goodbye, I am buried in the dirt
I no longer feel pain it is just that everything hurts
The value of my corpse is devalued and has no worth
I am going to forget everything and have a brand new birth

life goes on

Where is my husband?
Madam please enter any place where there is a sign
But I am tired and thirsty
You will be given refreshment soon
Where are my clothes?
Madam, there is no rain or inclement weather
i feel deserted. Is there a priest available?
Whatever religion you are, you will be given comfort
I have no shoes
The ground is soft
Who are you? Why does your voice keep up?
I am the "Pathfinder". Just trust in your hopes
Mr. Pathfinder, what if my husband does not show up?
You will be able to marry another man. Please keep moving
(The light fades. There is soft music putting people asleep)
Pathfinder: "To those who are still alive, please kneel and pray""
I want my children. I demand an answer
Your children have all joined up at the end of the maze
Does the maze have an exit
There are no dead ends. Follow your feelings and you will come to light
God: I am so pleased to have all of you participating in my contest
Pathfinder: God, please leave them alone until they reach a destination
God: I can ill afford to lose any souls. My heaven has been empty lately
Pathfinder: You will be satisfied with the results of this test.
(An alarm signifies something)
There are lots of people milling around at the possible exit. You
promised me my husband. Why are those angels all eating people?
(All promises come to an end. Life goes on)

each encounter

Thing I miss the most is not staying married and becoming an institution
I miss having a mate who nods in agreement with me during a situation
Like if we are listening to a musical performer and expressing a unified satisfaction on the song, simply by our eye contact
I have seen it happen to others
I am envious
I have no one to conform to
No one who shares my reality
I gave up a lot by getting divorced
I gained a lot by getting divorced
It is a trade off
My main goal in life is to find more and more truths that are scientifically and spiritually concurrent
My main goal is a search for knowledge
So many of my old beliefs lay refuted and replaced by new ones
Marriage is a lot of work
Being single is a lot of work
I am not gay, but I am an abstinent hetero sexual person
Maybe I am selfish by only masturbating, but there it is, I follow onanism
I am not an institution, but I am a bark on a flowing river bumping both sides of the banks and picking up what I need from each encounter
What did you think?

air we breathe

I half listen, at times
To advertising, mostly
We all live with a majority of irrelevance
Buy this, buy that, free shipping, call now so you do not miss this offer
These high pressure tactics do not work on me, but I am partially cognizant of sounds and words
I hear Shakespeare's words: Me thinks the lady does protests too much
I fight against belief as commercials espouse "Try to do what's never been done. To win what's never been won"
Bob Dylan song Only Bleeding (partial lyrics):
Advertising signs that con
You into thinking you're the one
That can do what's never been done
That can win what's never been won
Meantime, life outside goes on
All around you

There is an order to the universe that is inexplicable
Things fit precisely in a magical unforeseen method that we do not understand
The hidden languages of ordering in a restaurant can belie how we use rudimentary words like: Please may I have onion rings
The waiter is an unfinished person who has not completed high school
The waiter can never fathom how pyramids were built
Yet this souls was born with language skills that astound science
Abilities explained by Karl Jung as pre-born skills from previous lifetimes
Our media use methods to drive their point across without us aware
of it taking place
We are like soft wax that some invisible stylus inscribes us with
I can go on and on but will end by my hypothesis that there are more mysteries surrounding us than there is air we breathe

letters

Dear Father Mike Ferris Thomas and mother Helen Patricia Nihra Thomas
Thank you so much for your example and sacrifice you made raising me and three other children
I can never be as unselfish as you two were living your life and never hurting others
You paid your bills and gave so much to us and others
Dad, you took the place of being a father for your nine brothers and sisters after your father died
Mother you were the most beautiful of your nine brothers and sisters
I am proud to be your first born and keep your memory in my heart

Dear Scott
You are my beloved son in whom I am well pleased
Remember me after I am dead
I love you

Dear Staci
You are the best partner I have ever had out of three others
I thank you for taking care of my affairs and remains after I die
Be sure to sell my house and give the proceeds to my son
All the remaining money in the company bank is yours and you no longer will owe my estate for the money used to buy the house you, your husband and three children live in
You are aware that any possible royalties from sale of my books will go: One half to my publishers and twenty five percent to my son and daughter
God bless you and thank you

Dear Nancy
You have the distinction of being my ex wife for over fifty years
Sorry you still carry hatred for me that only you deserve

Dear Susan
You have the distinction of being my first child out of two

Sorry you carry hatred for me that only you deserve

Dear Anita
You have the distinction of being the first of three of my siblings
My best advice to you is to be who you are and I wish you well but wish you away from me

Dear Maria
You have the distinction of being the last of my three siblings
Sorry you carry hatred for me that I do not deserve
My best advice to you is to keep the memory of your only child and daughter whom you did very little to help with her addiction that killed her
She was all you had to love you

Dear James
You were my younger brother out of three siblings
You were right one time years ago saying to me: I was the only person who knew how to live right
You said it out of envy since you felt that you did know how to live right
You also said to me continuously that you passed close to my house on so many occasions
I am sorry you never found the time to stop
You are dead and may you rest in peace

Dear world and all the people I have known
There are more mysteries than knowledge I have attained
I am first a fool but I do not dwell on my mistakes
I apologize for ever hurting your feelings
I thank you for all your kindness's
And, I can only say about my life: Father, forgive them and me for we do not know what we do

eroticism

Come close
Feel me
Smell my body odors
Touch my skin
I am yours
An encounter of sense

Compare me to others you have known
I do not compete with them
I am only naked for you now

Do not look upon my aged saggy and old body with disfavor
I am but human and can only give you pleasure that keeps a memory

My penis is my source of life continuing
My breasts are male but similar to yours

I carry no fantasy that we are forever
Nothing lasts

Those continuing orgasms that we have
Are doorways to a great spacious time that includes past, present and future

You are the most beautiful woman I have ever known
I gently massage the space between your legs
That entrance/exit way linking humanity/evolution/
cunt of continuity forever
And I kiss those lips and folds of your skin to delirious distraction

It's all about

It's All About
It's all about choosing
All about using
The power we have for delusion

All about losing
Bout the way our hearts are not fusing
together in unison

It's not amusing
To have so much amusement
Think of the pain we are causing
Think about the way we are bruising
The sensitive people who are locked into believing
That there is still some good to a nation or a world without vision

It's all about the product they are pushing
Soap and deodorants that leave our thoughts in confusion
With the volume increasing
And the way Hollywood is falsley pleasing

The simplicity of thought persuasion
It's all about the sweet and sour sensation
The easy way out of points with no reason
Like living normally is some sort of treason

It's all about sound and fury
Everyone being in a hurry
Headaches - so much worry
A judgement with no jury
Our future so blurry

It really is about the place we fill in the pyramid of potency
Where we, on the bottom, carry the weight of other's impotence
That religion or politics or academics divide us by making no sense

That even our music falls short by repeating
Chords without accompanying
Orchestral combinations
Large sounds with soundless syncopation
Cantata-less circles of toneless intimation
The very abrupt end to melodies in season

It is all about the way love is ripped out of our equation
The lack of kindness in place of comfort so pleasing
It seems to come down to mass-immunization against elation
A serio-comic end to humanity as the earth begins its re-creation

eternals

Reality overlaps
Situations in the past
Repeat themselves
Characters change but events duplicate
We watch species become extinct, but earth has its own agenda
All conditions start all over from cosmic fireballs cooling over
 millions of years
Condensation forms into oceans
We crawl onto land
Regrow our bodies - arms, legs, torso
Our consciousness re-inhabits workable vehicles
We go from caves to communities to cities
Large population groups run their time and run out of space and water
Our spirits remain
Our inherent development blends into new habitation
In college our professor stated:
The only permanent thought process is our mind
If we are made to the image and likeness of a god, we are our own deity
And, religion aside,
we are our own mirror selves in an evolutionary conundrum
We thank Carl Jung for showing us how language skills are carried from one body to another
We thank Noam Chomsky for affirming us as eternal
What did you think?

where it happened

It was eerie passing the building where he committed suicide
in the basement
Gloomy atmosphere pervaded
It was fall with winter feeling in the air
I only knew his brother
I could sense his feelings as before or after he hung himself
The rope tightened as he kicked the chair from beneath his feet
He wore tennis shoes
His breath stopped and time stood on its heels
Life is sacred
When it ends, all angels in heaven pause and pray
for the soul of the deceased
I never discussed this incident with the brother
The dead man had two sisters that I had romantic ideas about
I never told the women or their brother
I continued to service the brother but the memory
of this hanging stays with me as a mood
I had simply by driving past the house where it happened

kindness

When generosity is extended to me, it is always a surprise
Especially when the giver is anonymous
And, I have no way of thanking them personally
I forget when I gift others
I do it often and I try to remain hidden
This mannerism is that my generosity will be acknowledged
by an angel or higher power

I try hard to be kind to people I hate, like my ex wife \
or neighbor who has wronged me
My ex did not directly offend me, she does that to all the people she
comes into contact with

Her nature is negative, overall
I do not understand why some people are bastards,
cause it takes the same amount of energy to be kind
Unkind people get less value for their buck
One of my favorite gospel stories is how the centurion was told by
Jesus: Go thy way; and as thou hast believed,
so be it done unto thee.
And his servant was healed in the selfsame hour.

It would be nice if I got a phone call from a stranger saying
that I won the lotto
I will tell you this:
My kindness is returned to me a hundred fold

life

Dear Carolyn,

I think of our entanglement fifty years ago
We had three years and we moved away from each other
I never remarried
You joined yourself with a woman
You never responded to my publishing over twenty five books
It seems how our understandings of reality expand within our lives to add to our old beliefs
We become more than what we started out being
There is an open end to our growth and it will continue to get bigger as time elapses
I think that even god grows by realizing all the souls that are available for emulation
God started out being tested by Satan wanting to be greater than what Satan was
God had to enlist Michael, the angel, to drive Satan out of heaven and give god comfort
Carolyn both us and god progress in time
as we become wiser and deeper
I see pictures of you on the internet and you remain as a tomboy with less feminine attributes that I imagined when we first met
I think your initial attraction to me was to fill in your understanding of male ego
You were experimenting and I was your subject
I was experimenting and you were my subject
God was experimenting and Satan was his subject
All religions of all time are experiments in what god and reality are
Let me tell you that peace and war are recurring elements
of what reality is
Love does not last forever.
Felix and Fanny Mendelssohn

Loved each other
And their love came to an end
Their death took them into continuing understanding
as they were reborn and came to new lives
The same with you and I
The same with god and all souls who ever existed

say that I was courteous

I carry this with me
Burden of sorrow
Make believe
Eye of blindness
Fingers sore to feeling
Yesterday crowds itself into mainstream
I never know if they even give me a thought
I do remember them by topic sentences
They are linked islands / rosaries / patched as a quilt
Today I pretend that things are fine
I rub elbows but never rub feelings with you
You go your way and I go mine
After I am gone, say that I was courteous
I will do the same for you

I will pray for you

I fell in love with a lady drinking coffee at my sisters kitchen counter
I do not remember her name
She was barefoot and kept moving her toes seductively
Her body language was beguiling
Last thing she did that turned my imagination loose,
was to touch my shoulder
I went away and never asked my sister for her phone number
She was sexy and attractive, but I am glad I stayed away from her
Next, I am in love with my doctor: Badea Elder, M D
She wears burka and is probably in her forties
The issue that attracted me to her was how she took my socks off
and examined my feet
She was so gentle and she exclaimed how clean
and odorless were my toes
I hate being so sexually frustrated
I am eighty one years old and my mind outraces my reality
I have lived alone for over forty five years
and never have female guests visiting me
I could easily qualify for being a priest or holy man
Send me your name and I will pray for you

eternal

I remember a story about Alan Hovhaness, famous classical musician who destroyed all his works and started over

His new music is expansive and lovely. It is Atonal, modern and very religious

I respected his decision to start all over since that is what I did years ago with a huge volume of poetry that I just threw away

Since that time I have over twenty five books and I like what I have done

I think getting divorced is like starting all over

I left my wife and family like the Buddha did to follow a path of spiritualism

Of course, the Buddha came from a rich family that could cover the cost of his leaving wife and children

When I left home I was poor and it took years to make up the money I owed

The feelings of my two children and ex wife did not come into my decision

I only thought of my feelings of being so unhappy in a bad marriage

I believe that the people we leave just have to make do with reconciling their being deserted

Earnest Hemingway started all over with his writing and created the Old Man And The Sea

Ovid's Metamorphosis was created after he was banished to an island as civil punishment

War and Peace was written by Tolstoy after he left home in search for his peace

Much creative processes are the result of individuals beginning all over

Mohammad rode around in the desert to found his religion. His wife took care of the children and his estates

Alexander the Great died at age twenty seven in a foreign land and he died out of loneliness for his love for his mother

Seven Story Mountain by Thomas Merton was renounced when he begin to study Eastern religious thoughts. The Roman Catholic Church never recognized Merton's new beliefs of a religion away from Christ

Merton was buried in the Catholic Abbey in Kentucky where he studied as a priest. His body was brought back from Thailand for burial in Abbey of Gethsemani, Trappist, Kentucky. His gravesite was non elaborate and simple. I visited it and tried to feel his presence to no avail.

Everybody ends their life with some major decision that may or may not reverse their lifelong thinking.

Some people commit suicide like Anne Sexton who asphyxiated herself of carbon monoxide or Sylvia Plath who put her head in an oven to die.

I have often felt sorry for suicides because they were not brave enough to face death normally

I do know that suicides must be reborn and live a new life where they reach a similar situation like their past suicide and they must make the karmic decision to overcome their idea that they can destroy themselves.

That is the reason that people start all over, to reaffirm their knowledge that they are eternal, like it or not.

Jody's got your girl and gone

Metallic
Soft
French toast
Peanut butter
Petaled blossom
Plush finger pushed
A heart palpating
Expecting
Black zucchini excavated
I rub her Aladdin spout
A genie appears to fulfill my wishes
Open Sesame
A cave full of dreams
A can of blessings
A tail wags
An eye winks
Arms entwine like grape vines
Bittersweet wrapped around my heart
I surrender under terms
A cessation or armistice lets all parties rest
I am self indulgent and tired of evasion
Raise your hands
Anything you say can be used against you
Would you like some lemonade?
Maybe a chocolate chip cookie?
Take your clothes off
You have a lot of tattoos
What do they all mean?
Why do you walk with a limp?
When I blow this whistle start singing the pledge of allegiance to the flag
Please,, smoking is not allowed
We will end this with a melted cheese sandwich and some pickle chips

Close your eyes and go to sleep
If you have a dream to keep
Bury it in your memory deep
Where mention of it will make you weep
Out of the darkness a light will seep
The sound of a baby chicken will peep
And lords and ladies will leap
Smoke 'em if you got 'em
Ain't no use in going home
Jody's got your girl and gone

leave it at that

My charity towards David has reached its limits
I buy him lavish dinners
I give him things when he knocks on my door
asking for salt, potatoes, onions, etc.
I have driven him to work when his cars are not operational
On one occasion I let him battery jump my car to his using my cables
I share my cigars and time with him
I make dinners and send portions to him
I always tell him to keep the plastic containers I put his food into
He said he liked the cup I gave him some liquids in,
so I bought him two with the snap on lids
He commented on how nice my incense is
and I gave him a burning stick and a package of incense
as well as telling him where he can buy it at what store
I hate to overdue it, but he always smells with too much deodorant –
just getting near his odor causes me to subtlety move away from him
I responded to his knocking on my door at three in the morning
and gave him the key he needed for the storage shed lock
For all I do, he never reciprocates or returns any favors to me
I can classify him as a "taker"
Blessed are those who give back what they have been given
I feel so guilty when he, once more, knocked on my door
asking for a ride to work
I said, David you have three cars in the parking lot
He said, his car is broken down
I am not sure what car he means
So, I simply said, no to him tonight and I feel squeamish about it
I feel like I am judging him, but I must take a stand
and stop giving to him
I feel less spiritual by refusing him, but there it is,
I denied him tonight and I will leave it at that

forever

Dear invisible god who watches over me
Accept this prayer from the heart of a faulted human
Remember my father and mother for sacrifices they made to bring me
into this world and keep me safe. Their blind unselfishness;
Their unwary love is a gift to me that I thank them for
Remember my ex wife whose unabated hatred for me is her own reward
Please bless my lovely daughter
and son who make their way in a world of shadows
Look upon my partner, her husband and their three children with favor.
Think about my brother and two sisters with your grace.
They are doing all they can with the understandings that they harbor
Please give thought to all my clients, past and present.
I do my best to serve them
I try hard to love my neighbors,
some of whom are inconsiderate and some who return love
I am fortunate to steer clear of ignorance
and have studies that keep me on a path free of distortions
The byways and entanglements of crime
and misbehavior are not my ways
The police sirens wail not for me
as they pass leaving me unknown to their pursuits
May fire and pestilence swerve around me leaving me safe
Lastly, give mind to me, your humble servant.
Smote my enemies with your fiery sword
swung in the hands of your angels.
Let my foes feel fear from your godliness.
Let all that I come into contact with
feel your unconditional love for all precious time.
I thank you for benefits that I rarely deserve, but accept with gratitude
You are god of birth, life and death.
I adore all that surrounds you, forever

waiting

These small things make up my days
Waiting for stop lights to turn green
Watching closely at intersections
Anticipating other drivers to be erratic –
They are human and get as distracted as I do
Waiting for my gums to heal after an extraction
Waiting to meet my oral surgeon
to discuss my implants and arrive at a plan
Waiting for old plans to be discarded
and new ones take their place
Life is a series of plans that the angels smirk at
Waiting for my appointment for cataract surgery
Waiting for my eyes to close as I slowly fall asleep
Waiting for my mind to become fully aware as I wake up
Wobbling on my feet as I stand from a sitting position
Waiting for time to reach late evening
so I can enjoy my once-a-day pipe smoke
Waiting for my ex wife and angry daughter
to come to some peace with themselves (If that will ever happen)
Waiting for my prescription for insulin to come due
so I can use the coupon for one free box
Waiting for my sins to be forgotten
Waiting for my good deeds to be remembered
Waiting for death to reach me soon
since I am over eighty and past due

words

Spring Summer Autumn
Irretrievable
Let these words embarrass you - Fuck your mother
I am in fear of Hitler, the bastard mother fucker
I do not collar Jews or abandon Polacks in Indonesia
The sharp sword could cut butter or be used for hari-kari or seppuku
Bring hate out into the open like a hysterectomy
You cannot eat nails but they can tie words together
I can bind you from moving but not from feeling
Do not open that door under penalty of eviction
A type of an enigma is a prayer to the devil
Wish for happiness at the expense of sorrow
Burning bridges is how I think of my divorces
Color me grey as my obverse image burns
Let it be known that I wish you ill
and I will feel better about my future
Ancient gardens sink in tsunamis
A catchphrase of wisdom is ignorance
Objectify that which is ephemeral
Look before you step backwards
A license to kill is another word for war
I cannot bother with triviality when extinction is imminent
Show me a poet and I will shred a stone

thank you

Allan and Alison:
I want to thank you both for giving me such good advice about my ex wife and daughter
The hardest part of thinking those issues through is: For me to get over the false guilt I feel
I truly have nothing to do with the hatred that they both feel toward me for these last forty years
We live our lives and work out the regret and the success we hold within our hearts
At age eighty two, I am fairly happy, writing every day, money in the bank, a good business partner as well as your and Alison's friendship
I have empathy to my son
I am a lucky man who works out the pain of getting old with an ease of physical ailments
I just thank you so much for the years of your caring for me
I have done all I can to give back to you two for the great books you have published
Reminiscence of my past are filled with always keeping on a straight path
And, I remember your words that objectivity and subjectivity are best framed within being reasonable - being rational
The best way to approach life is to love some invisible god and try our best to love our neighbors
Thank you so much Allan and Alison
My life is so much richer with your help

sacred song

poems
these are what comes out
of the vast reservoir of attentiveness
proclamations of ignorance
protestations of wisdoms
fanciful figurations
handful's of periods, commas, apostrophes weaving quilts of ideas
you will not know what is coming till it passes you like a train poem
a clatter of horse hoofs
here is a platter of roasted curlicues
let there be light
we will name all animals
give sense to sunsets
when you are in doubt, this will clear your mind
when things are confusing my poems will bring clarity
everything burning in my campfire will astound you
words are all I have to give a world of silence
sentences collected into parables
my prayer to a desecrated civilization is holiness
my gospel of diffidence is sacred song

understatement

There is no escape from the warehouse
Even if you get free from the packaging contrivances
Word will get out to find you and pull you back in by agent soldiers
I jumped between mechanical arms moving souls
from one constraint to another
The height of the storage pallets was infinite "
There was no sound
Total silence ruled
Precision was extreme
Struggles of other prisoners was felt but not seen
No appetite or hunger exhibited itself but endured unabated
Souls encased within particles where tortured quietly and totally
This prison existed without jurisdiction or any form of equity
No recourse for redemption existed
Guards were pitiless / merciless
Time was measured in eons
Most blood-curdling was the Chinese chamber of horrors
Nothing peaceful or serene existed in this scenario
Dante's Inferno replicated itself in one condensed layer of hell
Impaling was common
Those souls shut into bellies of sea creatures where as Ahab tied to a whale or Jonah sucked into a stomach of immense size
Woe to all who exist here was an understatement

regret

The room was full
Mourners saying good bye to Helen, my mother
Her eight brothers and sisters were wiping their eyes from tears
I walked over to the end table where there were strangers
who were all laughing and I questioned them
They were not relatives but hanger-on people
who had come at the request of my sister
I walked away and let things be as they were
I should have told them to leave and get their meal at McDonalds
Helen's relatives who were upstairs never got fed
since the kitchen did not prepare enough food.
My sister and brother-in-law would have strongly objected. I should
have told them that they had not thought through making the
arrangements holding the meal at their sailing club's small dining
room. The day of the funeral was very hard for me since my brothers
and sisters did not invite me to sit up front with them. I cried so hard
for my mother that I did not care
My brother and two sisters always have envied me. They try so hard to
compete with me without even knowing they are doing it. They never
went to college, they cannot write or think through complicated
concepts. I have avoided them all my life since there is very little I can
share with them. I care for them only as family ties.
Their children are very similar to them.
They are what might be called: The Salt Of The Earth.
In terms of my mother's funeral: Sometimes one has to take a firm stand
to make things right but at that time I was too timid and still regret it

Fix yourself

The three girls walked into Kohls

Counter clerks busy and ignored them

Marge, Mary and a third who just agreed with everything

Marge: Have any idea what you want?

Mary: Maybe

Marge: Okay

Mary: Damn pants keep rising up on me

Marge: Who picks your clothes?

Mary: What do you mean?

Marge: Need to get longer pants

Mary: Yea

Marge: In fact you need corduroy or Levi's. Some kind of designer brand

Mary: Yea

Marge: And, while your at it, get rid of that t-shirt and get a feminine blouse. One with some lace or frills. You also need some long leather boots. Maybe men will look at you, then. You know, Mary, You are not a dyke, you are college educated, a smart person and you need to change the way you look so you can change the way you feel.

Mary: What about you?

Marge: I am not like you or others. I am a writer, successful, have lived alone for over forty years and take good care of myself. I start out feeling good about myself, as opposed to you.

Mary: You are so opiniated

Marge: Good opinions Here is two hundred dollars. Fix yourself

Fuck you, to contemptible assholes

Things I hate eat my soul
Learning to live with detestation is a hard task
I wake up dreaming of getting even with people who are unkind
If I recriminate against them, I will become like them
I am spiritual enough to realize that all action comes back to the sender
If you are evil, evil will return to you / Kind and kindness comes back
But, nonetheless, it would be good to fix those bastards
Fix them by driving nails into their feet
or shoving a spear into their hearts
Maybe throw a rock into their windows or set their houses on fire
I am stuck with being kind.: It is in my nature:
Built into my character
There you have it
Even here on All Poetry, I never give bad reviews.
I read and just agree with each writer.
No matter how stupid or slanted they are,
I just do not argue with them.
Laissez Faire is my modus operandi
I believe it is the healthiest way to approach life
So, I will go to heaven or hell and take what I get for saying:
Fuck you, to contemptible assholes

Questions I would ask Valsta

if I took her for coffee or a meal

Valsta is a desk clerk at Vision Institute of Michigan in Sterling Heights
I noticed her and became attracted to her
My interaction with her has been limited to appointments and
information regarding my eyes and optical issues.
I did buy her candy as a thank you gift.

She is a tall woman. She is a full bodied strong looking woman. My
allurement to her is how she is kind and how she moves with grace. I
have yet to learn much about her but if I asked her out these are some of
the questions I would ask her: (Of course, there would be a give-and-
take, back-and-forth series of queries between us, if we proceeded)

If you do not want to answer any of these questions,
just ignore or scratch them off the list.
What is your full and maiden name?
How do you feel about being younger than my eighty one years old?
If you now have or would want a house pet,
what have you or what would you chose?
Where were you born, what date and time?
What city did you spend your growing up?
Do you like thunderstorms?
Do you like yourself?
Do you follow Astrology, Palm Reading,
Crystal Ball Reading or Card Reading?

What is your religious orientation?
      Christian
      Judaism
      Islam
      Spiritualism

   Agnosticism
   Animism
   Atheism
   Deism
   Determinism
   Esotericism

Do you believe in reincarnation or a heaven and hell?
Do you have children by your divorced husband of ten years of marriage?
Do you have siblings or a large family?
What is the level of your education?
What do you read?
  Fiction
  Romance
  History
  Plays or Poetry
  Magazines

What music do you like?
What art interests you?
 What is your philosophical be

What is your sexual preference or orientation?
  Straight
  Gay
  Bisexual

 Have you any physical impairments?
I find you physically attractive and very sexy,
do you like my appearance and outward personality?
If these questions are too intrusive,
do you want to end this situation and not continue any further?

Plea Psalm

Father of all families
Crush all my enemies

Squash them with your big boots
Yank them from their shallow roots

Ancient mystery creator
Having no imitator
No sacrificial traitor

Give me peace from all who hate me
Obliterate those with obtuse destinies

Dear Lord of invisible presence
Show thyself to evil noxious men

Tear their arms and legs from their bodies
Let them bleed and birds eat their flesh

Oh! How I wish for your to justify life
And destroy the hatred of my ex-wife

Let it be known that you are my fierce ally
Hover over me in protection as eagles fly

May I forever be under your protection
And, when I die please give me mention

before and after death

Life is almost over
Age 82
Death closes in
I want to leave something worth remembering
I want to go somewhere worth arriving at
Like Gaugin or Hemmingway, I want to end with a bang
I will be remembered as generous
As kind and open handed as possible
I will be remembered for my twenty five books published –
if the world is not destroyed by a meteorite or eruption
like the dinosaurs extinction
Does Beethoven and all beauty go away when all life is obliterated?
I hope it does exist somewhere where it is kept safe
I wonder if Shakespeare is recreated on other planets?   If so,
then he is real busy because there are so many other planets
for him to work on
I think that I would like to face people who hate me, after I die
I would like to ask them what they hated me for
From my point of view, I have done nothing to hurt other people,
other than learning how to become a better person as time went by
Maybe anger and hatred dissolves after death
when people understand themselves clearer
Or, maybe, hate continues on the other side of the veil
What exists below, exists above and what exists above exists
below (something from the bible)
This is a rambling piece of writing and I would not find fault
in you if you pass over it as trivial
That is the one thing I do not want to leave behind
or find when I die: To be trivial
I am important and will fight for my fame
or heritage before and after death

mixed up sods

I am blessed with all things from the Lord
What I use to survive and what I hoard

I read where others are deprived or starving
I do not see it first hand so I can be imagining

It is like the Lord being here but being invisible
Like Rembrandt's art seen as just scribble

My reality is something I keep inside of me
I present a face to the world for others to see

Not sure what is right or what is wrong
So many ways to view life as just a song

I will tell you this: So many souls are twisted
I cast them aside, in none of them am I interested

Here is what they do: They cling to false heroes
Instead of braving their own beliefs they are shallow

Like Hitler's followers they give up on truth for ideals
That are less than strong but weak as how it seals

So many dead ends where you can fall off the cliff
Missing the whole point of love, breathless as a stiff

Let me tell you, it is better to question and not be sure
Than to follow fake quagmires with fantasies of allure

Love yourself, your neighbor and trust the gods
You will die much happier than mixed up sods
What did you think?

incomplete

She was playing the cello
She knew Mary Ann
Said that Mary Ann just got high, but not on drugs,
but for falling in love'
We went to Mary Ann's door and knocked
There was no peep hole
Mary Ann did not open the door because her phone bill
payment was late
She looked through a small opening in the curtains
to spy on the people on her porch
Once, Mary Ann, did not open the door
to acknowledge Christmas carol singers
Something about a dream that is always incomplete

camaraderie

The job was finished
Jake gave the keys for the house to the owner
and walked to the two cars with Jessup
They examined the left over items
and scratched their heads cause there was too much
for Jake to load on the small Pinto

Jessup pointed to his new cargo van and said to Jake:
We will load it on my car and take it to Florida.
Jake was reluctant but finally agreed as Jessup threw his keys
to his friend and they started to move all the boxes
and long pieces of wood onto the cargo van

They tied everything down with strong ropes and straps.
Jake said: How is it that you have all these moving materials?
Jessup just shook his head to indicate he did not know
When they were finished, Jessup suggested they drive
to the nearby Office Depot and leave the empty Pinto
in a safe place behind the store.

Jake agreed and after they were done,
Jessup got into the passenger seat
to let Jake start the drive to Florida
Jake had a half finished home in Florida
where these materials would come handy

 "Jessup, you got a life and you do not need
to spend all this time driving back and forth."
Jessup just waved his hand and said: Let's go.
This is what friends do for each other

If he comes back, we will kill him again

It is Christmas day

Revelry celebrations of the birth of Christ pervades most of the world except for Muslim, Chinese and Buddhist areas

Often historical facts contradict long held beliefs

We need myth more than we need actuality to be happy in life

So, Mary is pregnant without the help of Joseph - A miracle that Planned Parenthood has no answer for other than she could have gotten an abortion so as to save face for Joseph who did not have Viagra each time he crawled into bed with his wife who kept reminding him that she was too holy for his urges

Myth has the Buddha being born in a similar fashion:

Buddha's mother, Maya, conceived him when she dreamed that a white elephant entered her right side. She gave birth to him in a standing position while grasping a tree in a garden. The child emerged from Maya's right side fully formed and proceeded to take seven steps. Buddha's dad waved his hands and said that was his wife's side of the story. He said it was a lot less complicated than how she put it. He said that her side of the family always exaggerated things

Pretty fancy myth, that also, Planned Parenthood has no answer for

At least Caesar and Alexander the Great had normal mothers as well as Einstein, Ptolemy, Euripides, Mohammad, Pythagoras, Ben Johnson, Shakespeare and most all other peoples who lived in history including Hippocrates, Imhotep, Albertus Magnus, Roger Bacon, Ambrose Pare, Andreas Vesalius, The Great Paracelsus, Our most famous Francis Bacon, Claude Bernard, William Thomas Green Morton, Joseph Lister, Pasteur and on-and-on with so many famous people who all were born with mothers

After Jesus was born his myth continues. We never are told who circumcised Jesus. We never found out if his wisdom teeth were removed or if he was given the Polio vaccination. We only imagined that Joseph and Mary gave Jesus a toothbrush and a tube of Colgate toothpaste. Did Mary take her son to the beauty salon to get his hair cut? The hairdressers probably told Mary that she had a real smart son. Mary never told them that he was the son of god. She wanted to stay on good terms with them

Also, history never tells us how Jesus had his finger and foot nails trimmed

We only read that Joseph was told to take a different escape route to Egypt since King Herod was on the loose to kill him and all new born children. Mary would not allow Joseph to purchase a 38 Special unless he registered it. He told her that he promised to keep it hidden under his toga where he kept his scimitar pearl handled dagger

Jesus probably went to kindergarten, middle and high school where he did not join the football team or play sports. He had his picture in the graduation book with the description of him being on the chess team and assisting the librarians

Then his parents chided him for hanging around with a bunch of dissolute fishermen who scrounged meals in the local restaurants. Jesus told them that he was part of the LGBTQ community and he refused to join the Ku Klux Klan

The local merchants hounded Jesus to keep turning water into wine. He refused

A lot of things start happening to Jesus and he had a secret relationship with Mary Magdalen and she filed for child support

Jesus was not dumb. He took an extended trip to India to study Buddhism. While he was away, Simon of Cyrene was proclaiming to be the Messiah and was hung for it on a cross. Out of this arose the great myth of Jesus being reborn to start Easter around the world

The world cannot accept the fact that Confucius taught to love your neighbor and love your government, two thousand years prior to Christmas

The gospel writers came up with "Render to Caesar the things that are Caesar's and to God, the things that are God's" And Joseph complained but kept paying taxes.

Jesus tried to explain reincarnation and the myth is that Jesus said: "You must be reborn to enter into heaven" Writers said that Jesus was speaking figuratively like Lady Macbeth saying "Out out oh damn spot" or "Macbeth shall never vanquished be, until Great Birnam wood to high Dunsinane hill Shall come against him."

We are told that Jesus will come back to vanquish his enemies and someone said: If he comes back we will kill him again.

a revaluation per se

Why have you come back?

To discuss something with you

Come in and sit down.   Coffee?

Yes please, I hope I am not bothering you
Do you remember how I argued with David over the story that he had read?

Yes

Well, If I disagreed with David, I could have been wrong. I do not want to get involved again with David over the issues on this one situation. I am not in need of David's approbation.

Okay

Lets assume there was a murder, as was originally discussed
Lets assume that we know the killer but we disagree on motives
If the killers reason for their actions were reality and their reality was based on their point of view, then, I have come back to tell you that I cannot find different reasons for their motives. It is suddenly become aware to me that I have no business to reinterpret the issues from my understandings

Very wise

Yes, very wise and simply stated: I must leave well enough alone since there are two realities: David's reality and mine

I have to give David the grace of his opinions without interference

I think you are on to something'

On to something or on to a redetermination, per se

Per se?

Per se. Succinctly stated: A revaluation per se. And I shall be on my way, thank you

be nice to me

I have two sides
One is get even
Two is let things alone (Lazio Fare)
I relish hitting back, but rarely do
Lead with the left arm fist and strike hard with the right
My dad used to say: Be cool.
Walk up to them close and kick them in the balls
At age eighty one, I never had to touch my enemies
My best defense is to "freeze"
An opponent gets unnerved by me going totally slack and not moving
In Vietnam I kept myself safe in foxholes
I remember my men and myself being flied into a combat zone to
process-in arriving troops
The commanding general said:
Why are you just standing there?
I said: Sir,
I refuse to work until you have dug us into foxholes
He did
In Detroit, growing up, I belonged to opposing gangs:
The Ravens and The Benny Boys
In High School, I immediately dropped out of the football team
and returned to helping Mrs. Ladenforf
and Mrs. McHarg keeping order in the school library,
as well as reading all the great books
By doing so, I got even with the brutes
who wanted to knock me down during scrimmage games
I talk a lot. I hope I am not boring you
Also, I avoided many sexual opportunities
simply because I was not interested in establishing weak relationships
Working for a large CPA accounting firm,
I was asked if I had fucked Vicky.
I retorted that it was none of their businesses
The love making came easy for me
Staying independent also came easy for me
I still celebrate fifty years of being divorced each year

Let me tell you my secret. I brushed my teeth after each meal.
James Yokum (same age as me) never did
and the bacteria went straight to his heart. He died at age forty

I have outlived all my enemies
Let me tell you another secret:
When depression leaks in,
I go out of my way to learn something new
and it relieves my anxieties
Let me give you a third secret:
I have spent most of my life in libraries or on the internet,
always doing research.
I get great personal reward for doing so
Another secret: Wish people well but wish them away
Never let cigarettes, whiskey, alcohol,
sex or an inflated ego ever become an addiction
Swab your ears with q-tips (gently)
and wash well under your arms
Sorry for having so many aphorisms
and keep reading my writings and being nice to me

television advertising slogans

I fool myself into believing I do not pay attention to television ads, junk mail or billboards

Truth is that the jingles and words are catchy and I find myself repeating them long afterwards

Its the rule of attention span and how we hear or see things

Like: I believe that my divorces did me no good, but I miss my ex wives

I would never want them back, like I would probably never buy any of those things advertised

I recently had cataract surgery and I told the doctor that: Now that I can see out of that eye, I realized that I had a wife and a cat

I told the doctor that after I have the left eye cataracts removed, I will find I have two wives

I will have to flip a coin to see which one I keep

My daughter once told me that she needed to hear the quick line of melody and words to a song so she can sing it to herself after the radio was turned off

Like, after we wake up, we need to remember a high point to our dream so that the whole dream will come back into memory

You know, when we walk or drive down a street, certain land marks become so familiar to us that we subconsciously remember where we are and feel secure enough to look for new items to place our minds at ease or locate us

I will tell you this: Our mind or consciousness is very complicated - more so than we can imagine

I will tell you this: Marriage was a lot more intricate that just spending a few years with another person

We are more sinner than we believe
We are more saintly than we think

There was a time when I wrote love poem duets with another writer on line
My wife, at the time, was jealous.
I could not imagine that she would feel threatened by two thousand miles between both me and the other person I was writing with

I think she felt insecure because she could not write as well as I could
She felt it a betrayal of our love for each other
I simply put it away in my heart as inconsequential, but there it was like an advertising slogan hidden away waiting for me to bring it forward like a television advertising slogan

We can only be human

We hang on edges of life
Little crevices of footholds
Dare not to look down into an everlasting abyss
Keep our teeth clean
Take our medicines
Cut our nails
Clean wax out of our ears
Eat good foods
Try our best to be nice to neighbors
It gives us no further time on this earth

We are born to die
Scream our last cry
Tell who remains
Did our best - tried
Place no blames
On third party ties
Life is blessed gift
Heal heaven hell rift
We leave earth cold
For warmth of gold
God's twice tale told
Adam and Eve scold
Their creator of old

Now, like it or not
We are all we got
Cain killed Abel
Tower of Babel

Language divides us

Basis of all mistrust

Prayer versus lust
Try always we must
Before dust-to-dust

Listen to wisdom
It's all we're given
Our sins forgiven

We can only be human
We deal with it fuming

she's all I adore

Thirst for Teresa ne'er slakes
She's the jim-jam-jakes
Gives more than she takes
Touching her gives me shakes
Eve's got nothing on her snakes
She rises out of funereal wakes

She is old but slides sideways
Comes unglued when prays
Better stretched out when lays
Makes me go upright in craze

I'm Christian gone to deviltry
Takes me out of eternity

She comes and goes
Like Marco Polo's
Got to be grateful
For her full hand-full

I cuss and swear
I come like King Lear
I am Achilles
Goat on Antilles

In music I fall asleep
With dreams to keep
Teresa, Teresa my safety in a shoal
A sea creature with a whale blow
A worm in the grass, creature of snow

When she dozes next to me I snore
A vixen, an angel, she's all I adore

with as little pain as possible

I've got a yearning
I'm still learning
Times during
Interludes

I will try to not be rude
Or come totally unglued

My heart is leaning
Toward forgiving:

Ex wives
And calcitrant clients
For not paying me
For services rendered
As a CPA (Certified Public Accountant) for doing their taxes

But, it is how things go
Nothing is perfect
Except divorces
Which come with much relief
Or, sometimes with grief

I could have bought a mansion if all the people who cheated me, paid

But, I am lucky enough to have stowed away a largesse
And I am careful to not lose it

But, I still have a desire
To reach much higher
 In a spiritual sphere

You know how it is: Overcoming untoward thoughts or actions
I have reached a decision to not endure Catholic confessions
Or even attending church services

My life is much less constrained in doing so

Let me tell you
It is a "rum-go"
Out in the snow
Winds that blow

But, now that I have had successful cataract surgery, I will die and be able to see god (without glasses)

Or see coroners hovering over me draining my blood or preparing me for cremation
It just fills me with elation
And I have, like Hemmingway, reached the end of my discourse
But I will not shoot myself with a shotgun
That, my friends, is much too extreme
I will just die naturally with as little pain as possible

repondez s'il vous plait

je t'aime
si tu m'aimes
si nous avons le temps
And, of course, if both of us can match each others passion
(le passion)
We will combine our wealth
And, because you will come out ahead, there will be a prenup agreement drawn up by my attorney: Dowecheatemandhow
Their phone number is 509 355 2931
Halte deine Hose fest
Hold onto your breath or Halt deinen Atem an
My brother is very jealous of our union and therefore he is not invited into our house
His wife holds his anger in check
His jealousy begin in school and has continued as time progressed
Paenitet me in confusione
The world is wide and varied and we fit in as best we can
Remember, each of us must sell their present home and move into a new home that will house our new relationship
Contact your CPA as I have done on my end. If you need mine to represent you, let me know
We must be sure there is at least a two car garage, minimum. I do not want to have to clean snow off of my car
I would not mind you bringing your two cats: Jasper and John, but, please no dogs - s'il plait
Lately, I have been concentrating on playing Robert Casadeus interpretation of Gabriel Faure's preludes. Be sure to not interrupt me when you hear the stereo
I will keep the door closed on the music room with the piano in it
I do not mind you playing Adele's new album since she lost all that weight
Thank you for reading this and - repondez s'il vous plait

our worth and growth

Patricia keeps popping up in my dreams

She died of so many things, it is hard to differentiate

She had soft breasts that I liked to touch when her husband was downstairs or out of sight

For a few months I slept naked with her but I could never get aroused enough to just fuck her

I told her that I was the type of man who liked to have his consort stay the night and sleep and wake up with her

She could not understand why i was the way I was

I think that was a problem that a lot of people had with
me: Understanding me

At this age of over eighty, I just do not care any more

For forty years, Patricia was close to me emotionally and physically

I gave money, time and energy to make her life as comfortable as possible

I gave and expected very little back from her

In the end she and her husband took and took from me and returned nothing

When her time came to die, I was estranged from her and it did not affect me too much

But, I cannot just write off someone who had such an impact on me

She was a spiritual advisor and conversationalist of the highest order

Despite her mental hinderances, she was brilliant

I used to laugh at her husband describing her as having a high school education since she overshadowed him in so many ways intellectually

I will end by saying this: No one person or thing defines us as we go through life. We are a composite of many incidents and individuals. We are, in the end, complete within our mind as to our worth and growth

earth plates

Oh night covering earth in murky silence
Lending shadows their deep significance
Come give me attending forgiveness

For my confession complete contrition
I am pilgrimed in a miracle oblation
Spun from evil's consuming gyration

Let there be peace in my soul forever
For all my effort and strong endeavor
None of life's wisdom make me clever

I give myself to consummate climates
Where god's grace-full love originates
Above clouds and below earth plates

graceful forgiveness's

Although you do not understand, I pardon you

Never is is more true that: You do not know what you do

Self preservation is ulterior to you as an animal response to impending dissolution

Your name and memory will be inscribed upon scrolls buried beneath upheavals of geology

Your progeny have been born watered down and ineffective

They, also, will follow a path of self preservation in a state of unawareness

Like a family tree tracing insignificant combinations, you will leave a shadowed reminder of how life can become desultory in some cases and become outstanding in others

Turn toward the magnificence of star clusters and the night will hold a promise of hope

Collect yourself into thoughts of redemption

The god would never desert even the lowest of creation

Remember the shepherd who struggles to save one sheep while the flock waits patiently

Remember the soldier who throws himself upon an exploding grenade to save his friends

Remember the man who walks ahead of his fellow prisoner in line on the way to execution

A crematorium leaves only the bones in its ashes

I have lived with your jealousies surrounding me like fat around flank steak

The meat will cook as the grease falls away

You and your line of evolution will become footprints awash on a beach of waves

The trackers who try to find your trail will come up short

And all that will remain of you will be my graceful forgiveness's

cry out of sorrow

Forgive me
For I have swerved away into a path of danger
Where the wolf of abject dissolution waits with fangs hungry
I have let loose the bowels of belligerence
Those nights of lassitude when euphoria covered over my awareness
It is in ignorance that we believe our pleasure is upmost
The pangs of consciousness wait to overcome us
Try to hide behind our sins and we will be stripped of defenses
We will become food for dogs
Give me absolution for my transgressions
I fly back into arms my god and cry out of sorrow

no one is perfect

Some people come into our life for a short time and leave long term memories

I did not know his name

He was sleeping in the laundry room on the floor with the temperature near zero Fahrenheit

I woke him and asked if he was alright

He was afraid that someone came to throw him out

I had no idea how he got into the building or that one of the other residents might see him

I questioned him and took chips, bottled water, a banana and an apple to him as well as a blanket

I left him for the night and before morning I got him up and drove him to a motel three miles away and paid for a room

I would not tell him my name or allow him to see my credit card and the clerk kept it private

The clerk knew he was a street bum and tried to be nice to him

Now, I could not go through the trouble to give him clean clothes or money for food

I would not let him hug me but was nice to him and went home, washed the blanket and made sure there was no other evidence of his presence

Life is like the gospel parable of the man who was taken out of a ditch and put up for the night

I just did what was right in my heart for this bum

We try to compare his plight to our lives when, maybe, we were down-and-out and,

How we overcame our deficiencies and straightened out our lives

None of us are perfect, but we learn by adversity

We sleep comfortable and eat well while some around the world are poor and hungry

We are lucky and thank some god for our benefits

God is invisible but the problems we face are real and we just do our best to be kind because no one is perfect

Spring comes from snow

Passing, not meant to stay
Impermanent for the day
Distanced as gone away
Sad, things are that way

We live edge of extinction
Like life is made of fiction
Sin without any contrition
Transgressions bitching

Some god made us as-is
Full of vinegar and piss
Against all we can wish
In a Greek-Trojan ditch

Yet we will yet overcome
As if a respectable bum
Adult chewing kids gum
Drunk on Spanish rum

So, just let all things go
Trust the wind will blow
Poor to rich with dough
Spring comes from snow

We come from dust and return to it

Everything passes into history
What is left is a memory
Of Jack Johnson
Mohammad Ali
Tiger Woods
Tom Brady
We are short lived'
The obituary column catches up with all of us
Sometimes we outlive our enemies or they outlive us
Sometimes we visit graveyards but the grass covers everything eventually

Archeologists both physical and social dig us up in fascination of how we compare to them
Sigmund Freud made us feel guilty for our distinctive differences and cast us into therapy forever
Karl Jung tried hard to make Freud understand where language came from, but Freud kept to his theory that we inherit it within a lifetime, not before birth.

Both Freud and Jung passed into history
Socrates left the earth under his own power.   Bravo to him
Whoever Homer was, he left us the Iliad and Odyssey as the first books of history
The History of the Decline and Fall of the Roman empire is required reading in all schools thanks to Edward Gibbon

Adolf Hitler did not last too long. He ranted and raved and expired even before his echo resounded around his bunker

The Jews represent 15 million people of a world total of 8 billion, yet their importance is greater than any other group of people in history

If the Jews accepted Jesus as the messiah, their history would almost end. They are still waiting for a return of a messiah and they keep wearing those funny hats (yarmulkas or kippahs)

Some wild thinkers, presently, are waiting for a return of John F Kennedy and his brother

Caesar would not listen to his wife and he was stabbed to death even by his friend Brutus

Shakespeare has gone to sleep forever and left us his great imagination in writings

Beethoven tried to compose after he died and never surpassed his greatest achievements

William James conveyed his thoughts through Jane Robert's book: The After death Journal of an American Philosopher. He complained that he led a lonely life of study and writing and missed the comfort of people in his life

Carlos Castaneda tried through his Teachings of Don Juan, to overcome death but died anyway of liver cancer that took ten months to kill him. The Yaqui Indian Don Juan laughed

We cannot outlive ourselves. We are like straw or corn stalks wilting in the wind after a harvest

We come from dust and return to it

prayer of patience

sound torrents of rain-exhausted thunder
out-cropping moon vitiating sun's whisper
brittle space of congregating stars
Venus conversing lust with Mars

doorway to heaven's blue atmosphere
unfolding origami-thoughts so clear
skeletal ancestors become flesh
in Einstein's soft quantum mesh

we are scientific anomalies
walking tall dropped from trees
earth is our instructional book
nature opens doors for us to look
e
do not be fooled or mistake the god
think hard but on ground softly trod

papa and the moon

papa don't crack his bones
hair like white chicken's
bleached eyes sad blue

mama she cares less
than those days gone

papa he laid his gun
against the barn wall
watched for night fall
crossed in shadows

can't tell the difference
tween grey cow patty
from closed back door

papa he turned old
like chipped paint
dusty leaf mold
won't buy more stars
or the sky empties
of all it's memories

papa will seal up his time
in his eyes no light arrives.

Nocturne to love

Evening clings to eyes
Fingers fold to emptiness
Across space dimmed stars salvage
what memories are left waiting for sleep
I am crossed in sanctity by passive breathing

It is all in nodding off to reverie
That calmness of forgetfulness
To put away the day in sachets
A perfumed drained to pillows
Where listing sails fold into night

My last thought is for ancient airs
Of slow streams wilting thinly as
Melodic serenades of Chopin

Close me into you as we meld
Like lovers who were famous
By degrees of drowsiness

Barbara Graham

I understand the meaning of indifference
to your lack of kindness or show of pretense
as whatever you have to say agrees or makes sense
and, in the end, I always walk away secretly saying to myself, "how dense,
to be her would be to be less than innocence
as a soul empty with no penance -
ghost with no repentance."

"Namaste!" She throws her hair back like gossamer silk softly winded.
I want her between lessons of love's blindness
as she bends to whisper to me, this prayer:
"Make friends with death while your alive."
How can I counter her allurement,
she is cup cakes in color.

Before we go too far, remember: There is no heaven.
Don't forget it. It will leave you breathless
to see the dark alleys,
other side of the veil.

Namaste, I always considered it an Indian word,
American, like she said it from South Dakota:
"My Lakota blood boils for you."

That put me to sleep laughing many a night
and I always ended saying "God bless and Namaste."

What am I to love

Too many promises creep over dark horizons.
Far too many gardens of brown leafless trees.
She sang a siren hollow tourniquet noose song.
Her lips curdled cider vinegar bitter kissing.

I, the fool, to her, a broken winged sharp-shin bird
she kept caged by love in expectant conditions.

Can you imagine slow acting poison? A descent
into misery with escape impossible.

Pull the walls down. Let the water fall over cheek
and pillow soaked night of sorrow.

What was I to her but an emptiness taken in small doses
caught in between my fantasy and her reality.

What am I to love but a pilgrim of regret.
What is love when love is not enough.
Tear the eyes out of our head.
Shut our mouth to never speak
Nor decree ourselves happy.

For the thin line of fame dissolving

Beside a serene temperament I slip into obscurity
Like the literal finale of a whispered mention.
If ever there was a family, I drove them away
Becoming merged within myself illicitly.

Tried by Anibus: Covered in indigo Christ:
Somnolent by Buddha chant: I glide after,
Being singular as "One-With-Instant'cy"

Ahhh! Do not give time its demands.
There are no excuses for gallantry,
Love was neither "here-nor-there" and
Neighborly-ness coveted a black moon.

Gathered up skirt-like over ocean spans,
See a shadowed Cyclops one-eyed dancing,
Implacable ballet pirouetted-prancing gait
And bow to darkness along a blue silence.

I was always in control
But never self assured
Like a Luna Moth
To Yesterday.

My daughter

It was not love
brought you open.

The hospital neon ceiling blinked.

Everyone watching you emerge, from the silver glucose afterbirth,
waited for that first cry announcing
Achilles at the trench
bellowing for Patroclus.

It was a quiet sigh of accomplishment
that clocked you into time.

Your mother became empty of you.
She just wanted to fill her womb
with silence and her heart to sleep.

Resolution of poetry

Let it be me emerging beneath the melting snow
with a poem that wakes the flowers up to grow.

The balm of spring breeze with sweet pollen
making noses tweak.

If you are reminded of elation
or taken out of rotation
out of line or time
by words of love
then I have
done my
best.

Let the light be brighter
the night much deeper
the heart so lighter
and my spirit rise
to heights higher.

I can only look past the veil of knowing
what signs of significance point us into a dream
where heaviness sheds itself with the flutter of a leaf
and all the old injustices become resolved by indifference.

smooth edge of a saw

in all fairness, look to the chumps who fly erratically under the radar
they make lots of money and buy expensive homes
needing cleaning crews

Amanda mops and vacuums once a week
Philip keeps the boiler room operating
I remember one chump who felt no qualms in violating agreements
the reason for his brashness: "I am a lawyer. Let them try to out-sue me"

we litigate
we do not hesitate
he who does ain't a councilor

money is a funny thing
it is only as good as what you do with it
people always want more
they have no idea of what to buy other than to satisfy their shallowness

there never was one person who took their money with them after death
the only thing we take with us, across the veil, is our soul
if someone lived correctly and added kindness to their soul, then that kindness is their resume

I have no idea which end of a pliers to use
the smooth edge of a saw cuts slower

here is my aunt Minnie
she eats but she's not skinny
her cabinets are full of food
it puts her in a good mood

my aunt Minnie lost her husband in the war
and she never remarried
because it was too much trouble

Gill Blaze

We both had same blood
Flowing thru us richly
From a distance we touched
As if under a pandemic
Life is funny when one connects with another
There is unblemished energy

Come to me, I cure your heart
Stand by me in a fresh start
We will outlive Cupid's dart
Falling off pervernial turnip cart

I miss you but our life is bound
It is a same sun turning round
Uproar without a single sound
Death outlasts time all around

Little Winters

Little winters sweep us into crevices
Windblown shivering
Collecting remains
Of our entombment's
In quiet ceremonies
Of silences

quiet self assurance

We all have bits-pieces of our egos
that we consider special.
Snippets of experience where we excelled
or beat the odds.
Regardless of our mundane existence, overall,
we save ourselves by these gems of remembrance.

It could have been the pride of parenting.
Maybe once when we forgave,
or reconstructed our hate into empathy.

The delicate balance within us that keeps us intact,
as we face the world, this is our true mental health.

We do not need approbation.
We exist within a vacuum of
secret faith that transcends
religions or psyches.

It is one thing: surviving a mortar attack,
yet it is important to put these things in storage
and go about our lives as if we will be able
to survive the final tests of our life.

Henry David Thoreau: "The mass of people lead
lives of quiet desperation." And, this may be true, but
I say: Most people lead lives of quiet self assurance.

It is our savings grace.

days of light

The beleaguered heart
is the heart of caution.

The confident heart
is the heart of venturesome.

We cannot be free of self indulgence
until we free ourselves from our self pity.

Color my memories in blood roses
laid upon the bier of my timelessness.

How often we return to the colors of joy
is how we color our remembrances.

Mellow is my soul
from having been
pricked by the rose
of love.

Into my dreams of her are forty years of happiness
buried beneath the trellis of sanguine mysteries.

Let this flower speak of love's nourishment
fed by the sun of secrets
quieted by the moon of blue.

    Love is entwined with the seasons
    as flowers follow the days of light.

My book twenty five

It is almost an anti climax
I have published twenty five books

All put together and published by Allan Emery and Alison Emery
of Shoestring Book Publishing

I bled my heart out in these books

At age eight two, I almost have no more life left in me
Time becomes a blur of experiences

I have outlived most of my peers

I can never get enough of learning
Never tire of music, poetry and fragrances

I have learned to overcome pain and refused surgery over and over
I have learned how my body can cure itself when I let it

I am not perfect

I have accepted reincarnation over a heaven or hell
If the Jews cannot accept Jesus as their messiah, well I wish them well
 They can keep waiting

Thank you all who have read or commented on my poems and stories
 Thanks to some invisible gods, angels and spirits

I have never seen you, but I feel you
 These forces are like a virtual reality

Life is a make belief series of events that change as we continually think
them through

I give you my sins and convert them to redemption

Biography

Writer, philosopher, philanthropist Michael Thomas is a long- time CPA from Sterling Heights, Michigan and a fine poet. We "discovered" him languishing in an online poetry site, writing who knows what to who knows whom. To our great satisfaction, he has taken to publishing his words, and the world is all the richer for it. Here he is doing an impersonation of a Detroit Mafia Hitman.

Also by Michael Thomas

ISBN: 978-1492297567

ISBN: 978-1500267889

ISBN: 978-1492776932

ISBN: 978-1495419010

ISBN-13: 978-1501063275

ISBN: 978-1507634387

ISBN: 978-1514174104

ISBN-13: 978-1329825413

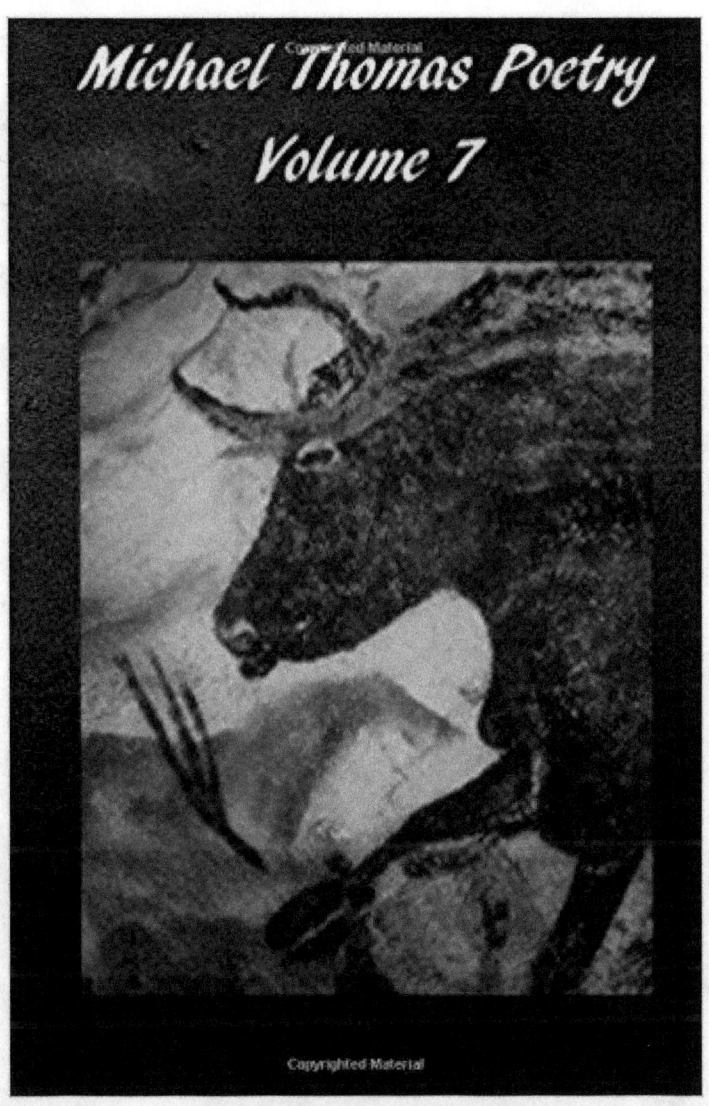

ISBN-13: 978-1943974139

Michael Thomas Poetry
Volume 8

ISBN-13: 978-1943974252

Michael Thomas Poetry
Volume 9

ISBN: 978-1943974160

Michael Thomas Poetry
Volume 10

ISBN: 978-1943974337

ISBN: 978-1943974832

Michael Thomas Poetry
Volume 12

ISBN: 978-1943974382

ISBN: 978-1530832071

ISBN: 978-1500192037

Rabbi Schlotz Talks With God

Michael Thomas

ISBN: 978-1943974726

ISBN: 978-1943974153

ISBN: 978-1943974221

Rabbi Schlotz: Street Talk

Michael Thomas

ISBN: 978-1943974320

ISBN: 978-1943974467

ISBN: 978-1943974344

Rabbi Schlotz: Loose Ends

Michael Thomas

ISBN: 978-1943974856

ISBN: 978-1943974894

www.ingramcontent.com/pod-product-compliance
Lightning Source LLC
Chambersburg PA
CBHW051838090426
42736CB00011B/1857